Material Matters
Metals

Carol Baldwin

Raintree

www.raintreepublishers.co.uk
Visit our website to find out more information about **Raintree** books.

To order:
☎ Phone 44 (0) 1865 888113
▤ Send a fax to 44 (0) 1865 314091
▭ Visit the Raintree Bookshop at **www.raintreepublishers.co.uk** to browse our catalogue and order online.

First published in Great Britain by
Raintree Publishers, Halley Court, Jordan Hill, Oxford OX2 8EJ, part of Harcourt Education Ltd.
Raintree is a registered trademark of Harcourt Education Ltd.

© Harcourt Education Ltd 2004
First published in paperback in 2005.
The moral right of the proprietor has been asserted.

Editorial: Charlotte Guillain and Isabel Thomas
Design: Michelle Lisseter and Bridge Creative Services Ltd
Picture Research: Maria Joannou and Alison Prior
Production: Jonathan Smith
Originated by Dot Gradations
Printed and bound in China and Hong Kong by South China

ISBN 1 844 43189 4 (hardback)
08 07 06 05 04
10 9 8 7 6 5 4 3 2 1

ISBN 1 844 43196 7 (paperback)
09 08 07 06 05
10 9 8 7 6 5 4 3 2 1

British Library Cataloguing in Publication Data
Baldwin, Carol
Metals. - (Material Matters)
1.Metals - Juvenile literature
546.3

A full catalogue record for this book is available from the British Library.

Photo acknowledgements
Page 4/5, Associated Press/; 4, Corbis/; 5 top, Corbis/; 5 mid, Art Directors & Trip/H Rogers; 5 bott, Getty Images/Photodisc; 6, Science Photo Library/J Amos; 6/7, Corbis/William Manning; 7, Corbis/Alain Nogues; 8; 8/9, Corbis/James A Sugar; 9, Science Photo Library/A Syred; 10, Art Directors & Trip/A Lambert; 10/11, Corbis/; 11, Gareth Boden; 12, Getty Images/Photodisc 12/13, Art Directors & Trip/M Peters; 14, /Tudor Photography; 14/15, Powerstock/L Miller; 15, Corbis/Christine Osborne; 16, Powerstock/ 17, Science Photo Library/Russ Lappa; 19 left, Science Photo Library/Crown Copyright/ Health & Safety laboratory; 18, /Peter Gould; 19 right, Corbis/; 20, /Jeff Edwards; 20/21, Corbis/Robert Essel; 21, Science Photo Library/F.S. Westmorland; 22/23, Corbis/Paul A Souders; 22, Art Directors & Trip/H Rogers; 23, Art Directors & Trip/S Maxwell; 24/25, Science Photo Library/Chris Bjornberg; 25, Science Photo Library/C.D. Winters; 26/27, Getty Images/ Photodisc; 26, Science Photo Library/V Fleming ; 27, Science Photo Library/ Oscar Burriel, Latin Stock; 28 right, Science Photo Library/P Goetheluck; 28 left, Art Directors & Trip/E James; 29, Science Photo Library/Roberto de Gigieno; 30/31, Corbis/Georgina Bowater; 30, Science Photo Library/P G Adam, Publication Diffusion; 31, Science Photo Library/M Bond; 32/33, Science Photo Library/ Rosenfeld Images; 32, Corbis/Tom Bean; 33, Science Photo Library/P Ryan; 34/35, Corbis/Archivo Iconografico; 34, Art Directors & Trip/G Horner; 35, Getty Images/Photodisc; 36/37, Corbis/Bob Rowan; 36, Trevor Clifford; 37, Corbis/; 38, Art Directors & Trip/A Lambert; 39 left, Art Directors & Trip/A Lambert; 39 right, Corbis/David Reed; 40/41, FLPA/B Henry; 40, Art Directors & Trip/J Ellard; 41, Getty Images/ Photodisc; 42/43, Digital Vision/; 42, Science Photo Library/ Dr Jeremy Burgess; 43, Science Photo Library/ Alex Bartell; 44, Science Photo Library/Crown Copyright/ Health & Safety laboratory; 45, Corbis/.

Cover photograph of the Guggenheim Museum, Bilbao, Spain reproduced with permission of Pictures Colour Library

Contents

Any words appearing in the text in bold, **like this**, are explained in the Glossary. You can also look out for them in the Word bank at the bottom of each page.

Olympic metals

Metals in our lives

Metals can be found in some unexpected places:

- in our teeth and their fillings
- in our blood and bones
- in soil and green plants
- in toothpaste and make-up
- in medicines
- in foods and tap water.

The metal magnesium is part of the substance that makes plants green.

The Olympic Games is famous for its medal ceremonies. The top three athletes in each event get gold, silver and bronze medals. But these **metals** are not the only ones that play a part in the Games and their celebrations. The brilliant fireworks at the opening and closing ceremonies get their colours from metals. The Olympic torch **relay** also plays an important part.

The first torch is lit in Greece, then the flame is passed on to thousands of people who each carry it for a small part of the journey to the location of the Games. For the 2000 summer Olympics in Australia, the Olympic flame went somewhere it had not been before. It travelled underwater along the Great Barrier Reef. Thanks to the metal magnesium, the flame from the torch was able to burn underwater.

Fast fact
The Olympic 'gold medal' is not all gold. It is actually made of silver covered with a thin coat of pure gold.

Word bank

metals   group of materials with certain properties
relay   journey where an object is carried by more than one person

Metals all around us

Many pencils have an eraser attached with a metal ring. This book was printed on a metal printing press. Many buildings have metal frames and so do cars, trucks and buses. Trains and their tracks are made of metal. Meals are often cooked in metal pans. Jewellery and money are often made of metals. Light bulbs have metal wires in them that glow and give off light. Glass is made different colours by adding metals. Our health even depends on some metals. Our world and our daily lives would be very different without metals.

On 27 June 2000, Wendy Craig Duncan carried the Olympic torch underwater for about 2 minutes, 40 seconds. After leaving the water, she passed the torch on for the next part of its 44,000-kilometre (27,300-mile) **relay** from Athens to Sydney.

Find out later...

How are metals made into sheets?

Why are metals used in glassmaking?

Why is the Statue of Liberty green?

Properties of metals

Shiny silver

When polished, silver can have a very high lustre. But silver tarnishes over time. The black film that forms on silver is silver **sulphide**. Silver tarnishes quickly if left in contact with foods that contain sulphur, such as eggs or mustard.

Pick up almost any **metal** object. Notice how it shines. **Foil** used to wrap sandwiches, silver forks, new coins and gold rings are all shiny. This **property**, or feature, of metals is called **lustre**. Lustre is a useful property because it means metals are shiny and attractive. Chromium, which has a high lustre, was used for many years on car bumpers and door handles. The ancient Romans used polished sheets of silver as mirrors.

Sometimes a silver fork or a copper coin looks dull. We say the metal is **tarnished**. Substances from the air also cause **corrosion**. But a dull metal can be cleaned and polished. Then the lustre comes back.

This silver kettle used to look the same as the spoon. It tarnished slowly over time as the silver reacted with sulphur in the air.

➤➤➤➤➤➤➤

Turn to page 41 to find out how metals corrode.

Word bank

corrosion   damage to the surface of a metal
lustre   shine that metals have

Pulling strength

Pushing or pulling causes strain in a material. But many metals withstand the strain and cannot be pulled apart easily. The small **particles** that make up metals stay close together. This property is called **tensile strength**. It makes metals useful as cables for bridges, cranes and lifts.

Engineers who build lifts need to know how strong cables are. If the cables are not strong enough, they could break. In metal factories, tensile strength is measured by a special machine. The machine pulls at the ends of a piece of metal cable with greater and greater force. When the cable breaks apart, a dial on a scale shows the tensile strength.

Titanium

Titanium is a very light and strong metal. It also has great tensile strength and does not corrode. Because of these properties, it is used in racing bicycles and human joint replacements. It is also used in the fan blades for jet engines.

The high tensile strength of **steel** lets these cables support the Golden Gate Bridge in California.

About 4500 kilograms of titanium are used in each engine of a Boeing 747 jet.

tarnish   make dull by a reaction with air
tensile strength   property of a metal that stops it from being torn apart

Gold leaf

Gold is very soft and is the most malleable of all metals. Gold leaf is made by beating or rolling the metal into very thin sheets. The sheets are often so thin that light can be seen through them. A stack of 10,000 gold leaves is only one millimetre thick.

Flattened into sheets

When people first discovered gold and copper, they found that the **metals** could be beaten with stones into different shapes. People learned to make jewellery, dishes and flat metal sheets in this way. Some other metals can also be hammered, rolled or shaped without being broken. These metals are **malleable**. Jewellers can beat copper, gold and silver into jewellery because they are malleable metals. Malleability also allows designs to be hammered into the metal. Some metals, such as aluminium, can be rolled into very thin sheets called **foil**. Aluminium foil folds easily around a sandwich because aluminium is malleable.

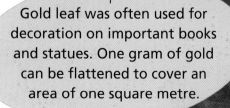

Gold leaf was often used for decoration on important books and statues. One gram of gold can be flattened to cover an area of one square metre.

Word bank   ductile   can be drawn into a wire
foil   very thin sheet of metal

Drawn into wires

Copper, aluminium, platinum and some other metals are **ductile**. That means they can be pulled to form a wire. Many metals, especially when they are hot, can be drawn out into long, thin wires. Most wiring in homes is made of copper. Covered copper wires are used for electric cables in appliances. Most power lines are made of aluminium. This is because aluminium costs less than copper.

How can a metal be made into wires of different thicknesses? The metal is heated and then pulled through holes of different sizes. Very thick wires are called **rods**. Very thin wires are called **strands**. Most electric cables are made of many strands of copper twisted together.

Fast fact
The thickness of wire is measured in units called **gauges**.

Musical wires
This guitar string is made of a core of metal strands with a different type of metal wire wrapped around the outside. The type of metal used affects the stiffness and the sound made when the guitar is played. Less stiff wires give a better sound. The most common metals used to make guitar strings are **steel** and nickel.

Sheet steel or aluminium starts as a strip about 5 millimetres thick and 1 metre wide. The cold metal passes through a series of rollers. Each roller weighs several tonnes. The rollers can squeeze aluminium to a final thickness as small as 0.006 millimetres.

This guitar string has been magnified hundreds of times.

malleable   can be hammered, rolled or shaped without breaking

We know this metal is potassium because it burns with a violet flame.

Metal	Flame colour
Sodium (Na)	Yellow
Potassium (K)	Violet
Lithium (Li)	Crimson
Strontium (Sr)	Scarlet
Calcium (Ca)	Orange-red
Barium (Ba)	Yellow-green
Copper (Cu)	Green

Conducting heat and electricity

A **conductor** is a substance that lets heat or electricity pass through it easily. **Metals** are good conductors of both heat and electricity. Silver is the best conductor. But it is too expensive to use for wires. So most homes and buildings have copper wires.

An **insulator** is a substance that does not let heat or electricity travel through it. Materials such as wood, rubber and plastic are good insulators. Wires that carry electricity from power sockets to home appliances are covered with rubber or plastic. These insulators stop people from getting an electric shock. Many cooking pans use insulators on their handles. So you can pick up a hot pan without getting burned.

Metal wires carry electricity from power plants to homes and businesses.

conductor   material through which heat or electricity passes easily
insulator   material through which heat or electricity does not pass easily

Magnetic metals

Many people use magnets to hold notes onto the refrigerator door. Only a few metals have the **property** of being magnetic. Iron, nickel and cobalt are the magnetic metals. They can be attracted by a magnet. They can also be used to make magnets.

➤➤➤➤➤➤➤➤➤➤➤

Turn to pages 42 and 43 to find out how magnetic metals are **recycled**.

Lodestone, also called magnetite, is a rock made of a substance containing iron. Lodestone is a natural magnet. The ancient Chinese discovered three properties of lodestone. First, lodestone could attract iron. Second, when they placed the stone on a piece of wood floating in a bowl of water, the stone always lined up in a north–south direction. And third, when they rubbed an iron needle with lodestone, the needle took on the same properties.

Magnetic Earth

The Earth behaves like a giant magnet. Melted iron and nickel flowing deep inside the Earth cause this **magnetic field**. Like all magnets, the Earth has two magnetic poles.

A compass needle is also a small magnet. Each end of the needle is drawn towards a different pole.

➤➤➤➤➤➤➤➤➤➤➤

Turn to page 20 to find out how flame colours are used to make fireworks.

magnetic field   area around a magnet where its magnetic force is felt
recycled   treated in order to use again

A bright idea

Tungsten has the highest melting point of any metal. It does not melt until the temperature reaches 3410 °C. Because of this, tungsten is used as the **filament** in light bulbs. The high heat of the bulb does not melt it.

Density

Most of the **metals** we use are very hard. Most also have a high **density**. This means that an object made of metal has a higher **mass**, or is heavier, than the same object made of another material, such as wood or plastic. The density of iron is 7.87 grams per cubic centimetre. The density of plastic is only around 1.5 grams per cubic centimetre.

Fast fact

The metal osmium is three times as dense as iron. A soft-drink can full of osmium would have a mass of over 7 kilograms, as much as a large cat.

Melting and boiling points

All metals except mercury are solid at room temperature. It is not easy to turn most metals into liquid. Most have to be heated to very high temperatures before they melt and become liquid. For example, the **melting point** of iron is 1535 °C. Most metals also have very high **boiling points**. Iron boils at 2750 °C, while the non-metal water boils at just 100 °C.

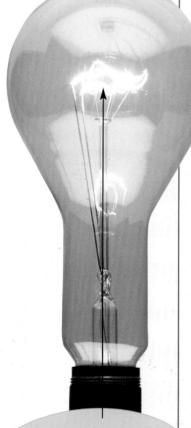

The filament gives off light energy as electricity passes through it.

Iron glows white hot before it melts. This molten iron has reached a temperature of 1535 °C.

Word bank   decay   break apart and change to something else
density   mass in a given volume of matter

Giving off rays

Some metals give off invisible rays and tiny **particles**. This **property** is called **radioactivity**. Uranium, radium and polonium are **radioactive metals**. The radioactivity of metals can be measured with an instrument called a **Geiger counter**.

Radioactive metals are **unstable**. That means they **decay**, or break apart, to form other substances. In fact radium comes from another radioactive metal. As uranium breaks apart, it goes through many changes. Part way through its decay it becomes radium. The decay continues until it finally becomes lead, which is not radioactive.

Dangers of radioactivity

The French scientists Marie and Pierre Curie discovered the radioactive metals radium and polonium. The Curies would show the brightly glowing metal to their friends at home. They did not know the rays from radium were harmful. Pierre was weak from radiation sickness when he died in an accident. Marie later died of cancer. It was probably caused by the radiation.

This symbol is now used to warn that radioactive materials are present.

---

mass   amount of matter in an object; in grams or kilograms
radioactivity   rays or particles given off by a substance

Atoms and elements

How many compounds?

Think about how many words are in a dictionary. All these words are made from only 26 letters of the alphabet. In a similar way, elements can combine in different ways to form many thousands of different compounds. The yellow colour in this paint comes from a compound.

All materials can be broken down into very tiny bits of matter called **atoms**. Most of the **mass** of an atom is in its **nucleus**. This centre part of the atom is made of two kinds of **particles**. **Protons** are particles with a tiny positive **electric charge**. **Neutrons** are particles that are neutral, or have no charge.

Ions

Electrons are the third type of particle in atoms. They have a tiny negative electric charge. In an atom, the number of electrons is the same as the number of protons. Their electrical charges balance. So the atom is neutral. Sometimes, however, atoms can gain or lose one or more electrons. Then they become **ions**. Ions are either positively or negatively charged.

Cadmium paint is a compound of the metal cadmium and sulphur, called cadmium **sulphide**.

The metal iron is mixed with other elements to make a variety of steels with different properties. These bridges and buildings have steel in their structures.

atom   smallest particle of an element
compound   substance made of atoms of two or more different elements

Elements and compounds

Not all atoms have the same number of protons, neutrons and electrons. Over a hundred different types of atom have been discovered. Each type of atom is the building block of an **element**. These are pure materials made up of just one type of atom.

Sometimes different types of element join together to form a **compound**. Water is an example of a compound. It is made of the elements hydrogen and oxygen, so it contains two different types of atom.

Fast fact
Atoms are so small that the full stop at the end of this sentence contains more atoms than there are people on the Earth.

Discovering the elements

It took thousands of years to discover all the elements. People in ancient times used nine pure elements. But they did not know they were elements. They used gold and silver in jewellery and copper and tin to make cooking pots, tools and weapons. Later, people learned to use iron for making tools and weapons. They also discovered lead, carbon and sulphur.

This copper coffee pot has been tarnished over time.

element   substance made of only one type of atom
ion   atom or group of atoms with an electric charge

The periodic table

Symbols of elements

Scientists arrange the elements in a chart called the **periodic table**. They are arranged in order of how many protons their atoms have. Hydrogen atoms have one proton. Helium atoms have two protons, lithium atoms have three and so on. Each element has a chemical symbol, which means you do not have to write out its full name.

> Some symbols come from an element's name in another language. For example the symbol for silver, Ag, comes from its **Latin** name *argentum*.

Chemical symbols are a short way of writing the names of elements. Symbols are either one or two letters, for example C and Pb. The first is always a capital letter. Some symbols are the first or first two letters of an element's name, for example Ca is calcium. Other elements have two-letter symbols that are not taken from their names, for example Au is gold.

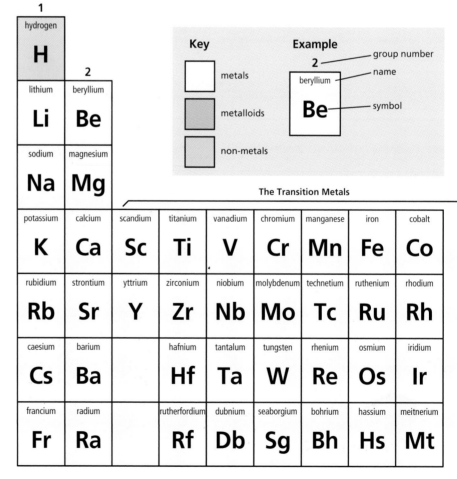

Key	Example
☐ metals	group number
◪ metalloids	name
◩ non-metals	symbol

Key example: **2** beryllium **Be** (group number, name, symbol)

1								
hydrogen **H**								
	2							
lithium **Li**	beryllium **Be**							
sodium **Na**	magnesium **Mg**							

The Transition Metals

potassium **K**	calcium **Ca**	scandium **Sc**	titanium **Ti**	vanadium **V**	chromium **Cr**	manganese **Mn**	iron **Fe**	cobalt **Co**
rubidium **Rb**	strontium **Sr**	yttrium **Y**	zirconium **Zr**	niobium **Nb**	molybdenum **Mo**	technetium **Tc**	ruthenium **Ru**	rhodium **Rh**
caesium **Cs**	barium **Ba**		hafnium **Hf**	tantalum **Ta**	tungsten **W**	rhenium **Re**	osmium **Os**	iridium **Ir**
francium **Fr**	radium **Ra**		rutherfordium **Rf**	dubnium **Db**	seaborgium **Sg**	bohrium **Bh**	hassium **Hs**	meitnerium **Mt**

Word bank chemist   scientist who studies chemical reactions
periodic table   chart in which elements are arranged in groups

Groups of elements

The vertical columns are called groups. Elements in the same group have similar **properties**. The stepped line in the table separates the **metals** from the other elements. All the elements to the left of the line, except hydrogen, are metals. Most elements are metals.

Metalloids

The **metalloids** are special elements that share some properties of metals and some properties of non-metals. They are also known as semi-metals. Metalloids conduct electricity better than non-metals, but unlike metals they become better **conductors** as they heat up. They are solids at room temperature.

Filling in the gaps

The Russian **chemist** Dmitri Mendeleev (1834–1907) made the first periodic table. He needed to leave gaps to make his table work out. He was not afraid to leave gaps for elements that were not yet discovered. Using the properties of elements around each gap, he predicted what elements in each gap would be like.

						0
						helium He
3	**4**	**5**	**6**	**7**		
boron B	carbon C	nitrogen N	oxygen O	fluorine F	neon Ne	
aluminium Al	silicon Si	phosphorus P	sulphur S	chlorine Cl	argon Ar	

nickel Ni	copper Cu	zinc Zn	gallium Ga	germanium Ge	arsenic As	selenium Se	bromine Br	krypton Kr
palladium Pd	silver Ag	cadmium Cd	indium In	tin Sn	antimony Sb	tellunum Te	iodine I	xenon Xe
platinum Pt	gold Au	mercury Hg	thallium Tl	lead Pb	bismuth Bi	polonium Po	astatine At	radon Rn
unnnilium Uun	unununium Uuu	ununbium Uub		ununquadium Uuq				

Gallium filled one of Mendeleev's gaps when it was discovered in 1875. Its **melting point** of 29.8 °C allows it to melt when warmed up in a person's hand.

---

metalloid element with some properties of both metals and non-metals

Groups of metals

Group 1 facts

- Although hydrogen sits at the top of Group I, it is not an alkali metal. In fact, hydrogen is not a metal at all. It is one of the elements called non-metals.
- Francium is the only member of Group I that is **radioactive**.

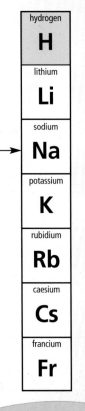

Sodium is actually more dense than potassium, even though it appears above it in the group.

The **alkali metals** are on the far left side of the **periodic table**. They are lithium, sodium, potassium, rubidium, caesium and francium. The **physical properties** of the alkali metals follow a pattern. As you go down the group, the **densities** of the **metals** increase. But the **melting points**, **boiling points** and hardness decrease. All the alkali metals are silvery solids with low densities and low melting points.

These **elements** are the most **reactive** of all the metals. That means they easily take part in **chemical reactions** with other elements and **compounds**. Because they are so reactive, alkali metals like sodium are always found in nature combined with other elements.

Fast fact

Lithium is such a soft metal that it can be cut with a sharp knife. It also has the lowest density of any metal. Its density is so low that it will float on water.

In pure form, alkali metals like this sodium are stored in oil. This is done to stop them reacting with oxygen or **water vapour** in the air as the piece on the right has.

alkali metals   group of very reactive metals in Group I of the periodic table

Uses of alkali metals

Alkali metals and their compounds have many uses. Lithium batteries are used in cameras and calculators. Lithium **hydroxide** is used in spacecraft and submarines to keep the air clean.

Common table salt is the compound sodium chloride. Sodium hydroxide is used in drain and oven cleaners. It is also used for making soap. Baking soda is another sodium compound. It is used in baking, to help upset stomachs and in some types of fire extinguisher. Sodium is also used in street lights that give off a yellow light.

Potassium hydroxide is used for making liquid soaps. Potassium nitrate is used in fertilizers and gunpowder. Rubidium is used in television tubes. Some 'electric eyes' that open doors use rubidium or caesium compounds.

Potassium in your diet

Potassium **ions** help to keep a person's heart beating normally. They also help to keep the body's nerves working properly. People need to make sure they get enough potassium in their diet.

Gunpowder is 75 per cent potassium nitrate, 15 per cent charcoal and 10 per cent sulphur. It is extremely explosive.

Bananas, oranges and peaches are good sources of potassium in a diet.

reactive   easily takes part in chemical reactions
water vapour   water in the form of a gas

The alkaline earth metals

Just to the right of the **alkali metals** on the **periodic table** are the alkaline earth **metals**. These metals are beryllium, magnesium, calcium, strontium, barium and radium. The alkaline earth metals are also very **reactive**. They are always found combined with other **elements**, such as chlorine and oxygen.

Alkaline earth metals are not as reactive as alkali metals. So some do not have to be stored under oil. Metals in this group have higher **melting points** than alkali metals. They are also harder than alkali metals. They all have a grey-white **lustre**. But they **tarnish** quickly in air. Radium is the only group member that is radioactive.

This symbol tells you that a substance is toxic.

beryllium
Be
magnesium
Mg
calcium
Ca
strontium
Sr
barium
Ba
radium
Ra

The red colour in many fireworks comes from strontium. A bright, white colour in fireworks usually comes from magnesium. Green in fireworks often comes from barium.

Uses of alkaline earth metals

The best known **compound** of beryllium is the **mineral** beryl. Green emeralds are a form of beryl. When cut and polished, they are used in jewellery.

Magnesium is important to all living things. It is found in the green **chlorophyll** in plants. Plants need chlorophyll to make their own food. And animals depend on plants for food. Pure magnesium is strong and light. This is why it is mixed with other metals in making cars, planes, spacecraft and ladders.

Strontium compounds are used in fireworks and in medical research on bones. Barium sulphate is used in medicine, in some kinds of paper and in fireworks. Radium is sometimes used to treat cancers.

Fast fact
Strontium and barium are usually stored under oil to stop them reacting with air. Like the alkali metals, they are very reactive.

Calcium is everywhere

Animals like oysters, clams and snails need calcium to build their shells.

Calcium is an important metal for many living things. Teeth and bones contain calcium. Calcium is also needed to make blood clot when we cut ourselves.

Marble and limestone are different forms of the compound calcium **carbonate**. They are important building materials. Concrete also contains calcium compounds.

toxic poisonous

Metals in glassmaking

Pure glass is almost colourless. To make beautiful coloured glass, metals or their **compounds** are added. Different metals make glass different colours. Iron and nickel make glass light green. Cobalt makes glass a deep, bright blue and chromium makes it deep green.

Transition metals

Transition **metals** are located between groups 2 and 3 of the **periodic table**. They are less active than the metals in groups 1 and 2. They are **ductile** and **malleable**, and are good **conductors** of heat and electricity. Except for gold and copper, they have a silvery **lustre**.

Properties of iron, cobalt and nickel

Iron, cobalt and nickel share a number of **properties**. They are all magnetic. Iron is the most strongly magnetic, while cobalt is the least magnetic. All three metals have similar **densities**. And their melting and **boiling points** are similar.

Element	Density (grams per cubic centimetre)	Melting point (°C)	Boiling point (°C)
Iron	7.87	1535	2750
Cobalt	8.9	1495	2870
Nickel	8.9	1453	2732

Iron horseshoes and horseshoe nails were first used about 2500 years ago. Until the 1800s, blacksmiths had to make each shoe and nail by hand, one at a time. Today machine-made horseshoes and nails are made of iron mixed with other metals.

meteorite   chunk of rock and metal from outer space that has crashed on to the Earth

Uses of iron, cobalt and nickel

Iron is probably the metal we use most. Some iron is used to make magnets. Strong permanent magnets are made from iron mixed with nickel, cobalt and small amounts of other metals. However, most iron is used to make **steel**.

Most nickel and cobalt is also used in making steel. Nickel makes steel more ductile. It also helps it resist **corrosion**. Nickel is also used for **plating**. This process adds a coat of nickel to another metal to protect it from corrosion.

About a quarter of the cobalt produced is used to make a powerful magnetic substance known as alnico. It is a mixture of aluminium, nickel and cobalt. It is used to make large magnets used in industry.

They come from outer space

Not much nickel is found on the Earth's surface. But large amounts of the metal may lie deep inside the Earth. The Earth's centre is thought to be mostly iron and nickel. This might explain why nickel is often found in **meteorites**. These rocks from outer space are thought to have formed about the same time as the Earth did.

The Hoba meteorite in Namibia is the largest ever found. It hit the Earth about 80,000 years ago. It is slowly shrinking as visitors break bits off for souvenirs.

plating   covering with a thin layer of metal

Copper, silver and gold

Copper, silver and gold are not very **reactive metals**. This means that they are often found as **elements** rather than **compounds**. All three metals are fairly soft. So they are very **ductile** and **malleable**. These metals have been used to make coins for centuries.

Today copper is mainly used in electrical wiring and home water pipes. Large ships are painted with paint that contains copper. Large amounts of copper are **toxic**. So this paint stops barnacles that slow ships down from growing. Silver is used for making jewellery, cutlery and mirrors. It is also used to make tooth fillings and film for cameras. Most gold is used in jewellery. It is also used to coat switches in electronic devices because it is a good **conductor** and does not react with air.

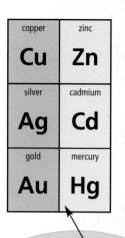

copper	zinc
Cu	**Zn**
silver	cadmium
Ag	**Cd**
gold	mercury
Au	**Hg**

These six metals sit near each other in the **periodic table**, but they have very different properties.

Slang name

Copper was used to make buttons for uniform jackets worn by police officers in the USA during the mid-1800s. The common slang expression 'copper' comes from this practice. The term was later shortened to 'cop'.

Fast fact

Copper jewellery and tools about 9000 years old have been found in the Middle East. Gold jewellery dating back to 4000 BC has been found in Egypt.

This X-ray shows gold fillings in teeth at the back of the mouth. One of these teeth still has a hole, shown in red.

Zinc, cadmium and mercury

Zinc, cadmium and mercury are all metals with a silvery **lustre**. But zinc is hard and not very malleable, while cadmium is soft enough to cut with a knife. And mercury is a very dense liquid.

Zinc is often used to plate other metals, such as iron. It is also used in batteries for torches, clocks and CD players. Cadmium is used to **plate** other metals and to make nicad batteries. These batteries can be recharged over and over again. Some common household products that contain mercury include thermostats, silent wall switches and **fluorescent** light bulbs. Mercury vapour is used in some street lights. It gives off a bright, bluish-white light.

Fast fact
The chemical symbol for mercury, Hg, came from the **Latin** word *hydragyrum*, which means 'liquid silver'.

Odd one out
Mercury is the only metal that is a liquid at room temperature. It is a liquid because its **melting point** is −39 °C. That is much lower than all other metals. Mercury would not even become solid in a freezer.

This blob of mercury is so toxic that just touching it could make a person very ill. Mercury **evaporates** easily, and breathing this gas is even more dangerous.

Traces of iron and titanium make sapphires blue. Sapphires are only found in seven countries, including Australia and Montana in the USA.

Aluminium

Aluminium is the most common **metal** in the Earth's **crust**. As a pure metal, it has a low **density** and is a good **conductor** of electricity. It is also strong. These **properties** make it useful in many products. Because it is both strong and lightweight, it is used to build aeroplanes. Aluminium is also used to make soft-drink cans, **foil** wrap and cooking pans. Drinks in aluminium cans can be cooled quickly because aluminium is such a good conductor of heat.

Aluminium's silvery **lustre** changes to a powdery grey layer when it combines with oxygen in the air. This thin coating does not flake off. So it protects the aluminium against further reaction with oxygen.

Fast fact

The **melting point** of aluminium is 660 °C. If an aluminium pan of water on a gas or electric hob boils dry, the pan could get hot enough to melt.

crust   outer layer of the Earth; we live on the Earth's crust

Lead

Lead is a fairly soft, very **malleable**, dull-grey metal. But lead is also **toxic**. Lead is used in storage batteries for cars and trucks. Lead is also an important part of **solder**. Solder is used for making electrical connections in circuit boards for computers and television sets. In fact, every television set and computer contains about 225 grams of lead. New types of lead-free solder are being invented because lead from old circuit boards is harmful to people and the environment.

Lead also absorbs radiation very well, so the dense metal can be used as a radiation shield. Doctors use lead aprons to protect their patients during X-rays. Lead is also used to shield X-ray equipment and nuclear reactors.

The solder used in circuit boards is about 40 per cent lead and 60 per cent tin.

Many homes built before 1978 had lead-based paint. When lead paint gets old, it peels and chips fall off. Many young children picked up the paint chips and put them in their mouths. Some got lead poisoning, which can cause damage to the brain and nerves. Thankfully, today's paints do not contain lead.

Fast fact

The ancient Romans used lead pipes to carry water. In fact the word *plumbing* comes from the **Latin** word for lead, which was *plumbum*. Some people think that lead in the water system poisoned many Romans.

solder   alloy that can be melted and used to join or mend metal parts

From mines to manufacturing

Panning for gold

Miners often pan for gold in streams. Gold is about nine times as dense as sand or gravel. Miners swirl water and sand containing gold around in shallow pans. Sand and gravel wash over the rim of the pan, leaving the heavier gold dust behind.

Gold was one of the first **metals** used by people. Gold is often found in its pure form in the Earth's **crust**. It was probably noticed because of its high **lustre**. Gold is an example of the metals that are not very **reactive**. These metals do not form **compounds** easily and are called **native metals**. Gold and platinum are common native metals. Copper and silver are more reactive than gold and platinum. But a few deposits of native copper and silver have also been found.

Gold is often found naturally in lumps called nuggets. This one weighs 0.5 kilograms. The largest gold nugget ever found had a **mass** of more than 70 kilograms. That is as much as a medium-sized man. The nugget was found in 1869 in Australia. It was melted down into gold bars.

This man is panning for gold in California in the USA.

Word bank   fluoresce   give off light when certain rays strike it
native metal   metal that is found naturally in its pure form

Ore metals

Most metals are found as **ores**. An ore is a metal found combined with another **element**. Usually the ores are compounds of a metal and one or more non-metals. Many ores are metal combined with oxygen or sulphur. An ore of metal combined with oxygen is called an **oxide**. An ore of metal combined with sulphur is called a **sulphide**. A **carbonate** ore is metal combined with carbon and oxygen.

Common ores

Metal	Name of ore	Chemical name
aluminium	bauxite	aluminium oxide
copper	chalcocite cuprite	copper sulphide copper oxide
iron	hematite siderite	iron oxide iron carbonate
lead	galena	lead sulphide
mercury	cinnabar	mercury sulphide
zinc	zincite zincblende	zinc oxide zinc sulphide

Glowing ores

A few ores will glow, or **fluoresce** (pronounced floor-ess) when **ultraviolet light** is shone on them. Willemite is an ore of zinc. If it contains traces of manganese, it glows a bright yellowish-green.

Fast fact

Because platinum is so unreactive, it will not react with chemicals in the human body. This makes it useful for pacemakers. They are put into the bodies of people with heart problems to make sure the heart keeps a steady rhythm.

Scheelite is a major ore of the metal tungsten. It is found in many colours, from orange to green. This piece was found in a mine in Brazil.

- Surface mines destroy forests and other habitats.
- Plants and animals lose their homes.
- Flooding may happen because there are no plants to soak up rain water.
- Streams, rivers and lakes may be clouded by soil washed from mines.

Mining

Mining is the process of removing **metals** or their **ores** from the ground. The method used depends on several things. Is the metal or ore near the Earth's surface? Or is it deep underground? Is it hard so that it needs to be crushed? Is the metal or ore bunched together in a **vein** or is it scattered?

Open-pit mining

Open-pit mining is used for very large amounts of ore. Soil and rocks are removed from above the ore to form a huge open pit. Pits can be from 30 metres to more than 900 metres deep. The mining is done with huge drills or by blasting the rock with explosives. Sometimes a whole mountain is removed. The ore is then carried up in huge trucks or on conveyor belts.

Most of the world's gold is mined in South Africa. In the USA, most gold is mined in Nevada and South Dakota. There are also three working gold mines in Wales.

Open-pit mining leaves ugly scars on a landscape. This is a copper mine in Arizona, in the USA.

hoist   equipment for lifting up heavy loads
mineral   non-living solid material from the Earth

Opencast mining

Opencast mining is another kind of surface mining. Here the top layer of the Earth's surface is scraped away. Opencast mining is usually used to mine ores that are close to the surface and where the rocks are not hard. Opencast mining does not leave holes as deep as open-pit mining.

Shaft mining

In shaft mining, a tunnel is sometimes dug into the side of a mountain. Most often, a **shaft** is dug down deep into the ground. From the shaft, tunnels are dug out in different directions. The ore is drilled or blasted into chunks. Then the chunks are removed from the mine by mine cars or by **hoists** pulled up the mineshaft.

Damage from shaft mining

- When **minerals** react with water in mine shafts, acids may form.
- This polluted water may drain into streams and ponds.
- Plants and animals living in the water may be killed.
- People can no longer use the water.

Almost nothing can live in water that has been damaged by mining. This stream in Manchester, in the UK, has been polluted by iron **oxide** leakage from disused coal mines.

shaft   vertical hole in the ground
vein   crack in rock filled with a metal or an ore

Metallurgy

Metallurgy is the science of removing metals from their ores. It started about 6000 years ago in the Middle East. Copper was the first metal to be used. The remains of copper mines have been found throughout the Middle East.

This abandoned copper mine is in Kenecott, Alaska.

Getting the pure metal

Ores are **compounds**. That means that **chemical reactions** are needed to separate pure **metals** from their ores. Chemical reactions require energy. This energy is usually heat or electricity.

Smelting

We can get metals from ores by using heat. This is called **smelting**. This process is used to separate metals from **oxide** ores. Iron is separated from the oxygen in its ore by heating it with **coke**. Coke is a form of carbon made from coal. When coke is heated, it produces carbon monoxide gas. This gas combines with the oxygen in the ore to form carbon dioxide gas. The iron is left over.

◀ ◀ ◀ ◀ ◀ ◀ ◀ ◀ ◀

Turn back to page 28 where the different ores are described.

chemical reaction   change that forms new substances with new properties
coke   form of carbon made from coal

Roasting

Two steps are needed to remove a metal from a **sulphide** or **carbonate** ore. First the ore is heated in air to produce an oxide. This is called **roasting**. For example, suppose lead sulphide is roasted. Oxygen in the air replaces the sulphur in the ore. The new ore is lead oxide. Then the smelting process can be used to separate the lead from its oxide ore.

Electrolysis

Magnesium and sodium are usually found as chloride ores. In each case, the metal can be separated from its ore by using **electrolysis**. The ore is melted with high heat in a special container. A current of electricity is passed through the molten ore and causes the metal **ions** and chloride ions to separate.

Ore from the ocean

There are lumps of metal ores on the seabed. The lumps, called **nodules**, are about the size of a fist. The metals in these nodules include manganese, iron, copper and nickel. Not many nodules are taken from the ocean bottom. It is cheaper to mine metals on land.

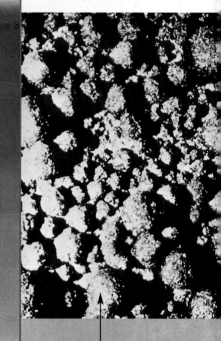

A blast furnace changes iron oxide to iron. Ninety per cent of the iron in the ore is melted and becomes what is called pig iron.

Fast fact
Roasting a carbonate ore produces an oxide and carbon dioxide gas.

These manganese nodules lie almost 5 kilometres (3 miles) under the Pacific Ocean.

electrolysis   using electricity to separate an ore that has been melted
nodule   small, rounded lump

Alloys

Many common **metals** that people use are not pure **elements**. Instead, they are **alloys**. An alloy is a mixture of a metal and one or more other elements. An alloy has **properties** that are different from the properties of the elements in it. Pure gold is shiny and expensive. But it is soft and bends easily. Copper is duller and less expensive than gold. But copper is much harder. Adding copper to gold makes an alloy that is more useful for jewellery than pure gold.

How pure?

Pure gold is called 24-**carat** gold. An alloy that has 92 per cent gold and 8 per cent copper is called 22-carat gold. This gold is used in coins. Jewellery is often made from 14-carat gold. It contains 58 per cent gold and 42 per cent copper.

Musical alloy

Marching bands have trumpets, trombones and tubas. These instruments are called the brass section. Brass is an alloy of copper and zinc. Its attractive golden colour and resistance to **corrosion** make it perfect for making instruments.

Brass alloys can contain different amounts of copper and zinc. The brass in musical instruments is about 80 per cent copper and 20 per cent zinc.

alloy   metal formed by mixing together two or more melted metals
Bronze Age   period of history from about 3500 B.C.E. to about 1000 B.C.E.

The first alloy

About 5000 years ago, people discovered that a new material could be made by mixing melted copper and tin. The new material was the first alloy, called bronze. It is stronger and lasts longer than either copper or tin. The alloy was so widely used that a 2000-year period of history is called the **Bronze Age**. The Bronze Age ended when people discovered how to use iron. Iron is harder and tougher than bronze.

Pewter

In ancient times, people made pewter from tin, copper and lead. The Egyptians, Chinese and Persians first used it over 2000 years ago. Dishes, plates, bowls and cups were made from pewter.

The problem with pewter was the lead. Lead is a poisonous metal. It was eventually replaced with other metals, such as zinc, bismuth and antimony. This new pewter is harder and shinier.

When a nickel is not nickel

Some Canadian and US coins are called nickels. But they are actually made of an alloy of copper and nickel. The alloy is mostly copper. Only about 25 per cent is nickel.

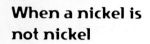

People used bronze tools and weapons before they learned how to smelt iron. These bronze arrowheads were found in Gerona, Spain. They were made over 4000 years ago.

In the UK, 'silver' coins like the ten pence piece are also made from a copper-nickel alloy. They do not contain any silver.

carat   measurement of the amount of gold in an alloy

35

Putting out fires

An alloy called Wood's Metal is made of bismuth, lead, tin and cadmium. Its **melting point** is only 70 °C. It is used in overhead sprinklers. When exposed to an unusual amount of heat, the alloy will melt. This switches the sprinklers on.

Steel alloys

Steel is one of the most useful **alloys**. Steel is an alloy of iron with a small amount of carbon added. Some steel also contains small amounts of other **metals**, such as chromium and nickel.

Nickel steel contains from 2 to 5 per cent nickel. This steel does not corrode easily so it is used to make gears and cables. Stainless steel contains 7 to 9 per cent nickel and 14 to 19 per cent chromium. It is strong and does not corrode easily. For this reason, it is used to make kitchen utensils and medical instruments. Manganese steel contains 10 to 18 per cent manganese. It is used in railway tracks and armour **plating** for military tanks because it is very hard.

Automatic sprinklers are often found in offices, schools and public buildings.

shape memory alloy   alloy that returns to its original shape when heated

SMAs

A **shape memory alloy**, or SMA, is formed into a certain shape. It can later be bent into a new shape. But it will always return to its original shape when heated. The most common SMA is made from nickel and titanium. So why are SMAs useful? Suppose a person has a blocked blood vessel. An SMA tube is crushed, then inserted into the blocked vessel. It will change back to is original shape at a temperature close to that of the human body. So once it is in place and warms up, the metal tube expands to open the blocked blood vessel. SMA are also used in braces to help straighten teeth and to join the ends of broken bones.

SMAs in space

Shape memory alloys were developed by NASA for the space industry. One of their first uses was in a large radio antenna. The antenna was folded up during the launch into space. Once in orbit, the SMA absorbed heat and the antenna unfolded into its original shape.

This chainsaw's cutting edge is made from a special steel alloy that contains chromium and tungsten. The alloy keeps its sharp, hard edge even though it heats up during cutting.

Although SMAs are very reliable, they are still expensive to make and not as long-lasting as alloys like steel.

---

steel   alloy of iron with a small amount of carbon added; some steel also contains small amounts of other metals

Metals and their reactions

The reactivity series

The higher a metal is in the series, the more reactive it is. This means its reaction will be faster and produce more heat. Metals above aluminium displace hydrogen from cold water. Metals above tin displace hydrogen from steam if they are heated. Metals above lead displace hydrogen from acids.

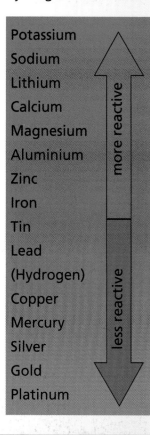

Potassium
Sodium
Lithium
Calcium
Magnesium
Aluminium
Zinc
Iron
Tin
Lead
(Hydrogen)
Copper
Mercury
Silver
Gold
Platinum

more reactive

less reactive

A series of **chemical reactions** starts a car's engine and keeps it running. Hundreds of chemical reactions take place inside our bodies as we digest foods. **Metals** also take part in many kinds of chemical reactions. New substances are formed by chemical reactions. The new substances that are formed have different physical and chemical **properties** from the original **reactants**.

Metals and water

Most common metals do not react with water. However, the **alkali metals** are very **reactive**. Lithium, sodium, potassium, rubidium and caesium (the Group 1 metals) react violently with water to produce a **hydroxide compound** and hydrogen gas. These metals cannot be stored with air around them. Air contains **water vapour** which would react with the metals. Instead these metals are stored under oil to stop them from reacting.

Potassium reacts with water to produce hydrogen gas. So much heat is produced that the gas catches fire and burns with a violet flame.

Word bank   arthritis   painful swelling of the joints
hydroxide   compound containing a metal and an oxygen-hydrogen group

The alkaline earth metals are not as reactive as alkali metals so most do not have to be stored under oil. However, the alkaline earth metals do react with water and produce hydroxide solutions. Some alkaline earth metals will react slowly with cold water. Beryllium will not react with hot water or steam even if heated to **red heat**.

Metals and acids

Some metals react with acids while others do not. The reactivity series shows which metals react with acids. Any metal listed above hydrogen will react with an acid to produce hydrogen gas. Those metals closer to the top of the list react more quickly. So hydrogen gas bubbles will be given off faster when magnesium reacts with an acid than when tin reacts with an acid. Any metal below hydrogen in the chart will not react with an acid to produce hydrogen gas.

As this zinc reacts with dilute hydrochloric acid, bubbles of hydrogen gas are formed and rise to the surface.

People wear copper bracelets to treat symptoms of **arthritis**.

Turning green

We release chemicals from our bodies in our sweat all the time. These chemicals are weak acids and will corrode the surface of a copper bracelet. A green copper salt forms on the bracelet. It can rub off onto a person's skin, causing a green stain.

reactant   something taking part in a chemical reaction
red heat   heat at which a material glows red

Metals and oxygen

In 1789, the French **chemist** Antoine Lavoisier discovered what happened when mercury was heated. He saw the silvery, liquid **metal** slowly change to a red powder. He realized that the metal had combined with oxygen from the air to form a new **compound**. That compound was mercury **oxide**. Most metals will form oxides when heated in the presence of oxygen. Iron **oxidizes**, or rusts, slowly even when not heated. More active metals, like sodium, react more quickly in air.

Oxides of metals such as aluminium and iron are used as **abrasives**. These oxides are used to clean and polish the surface of other substances like glass lenses.

Protecting iron

Galvanized iron does not rust. This is because it has been dipped into melted zinc. After being dipped, a thin coat of zinc sticks to the iron. Zinc does not **corrode** when it is in contact with the air. So it protects the iron.

Fast fact

Oxygen was discovered by the British scientist Joseph Priestley when he heated mercury oxide to form mercury and oxygen.

When iron comes into contact with water and oxygen from the air, the iron reacts with oxygen to form rust.

Galvanizing works because zinc is above iron in the reactivity series, so it reacts with the air first.

abrasive   substance that grinds or polishes a surface
galvanized   covered with a thin coating of zinc to prevent rusting

Extra oxygen

Most metals form oxides when they react with oxygen. But a few also form **peroxides**. Peroxides have an extra oxygen **atom** in the compound. Sodium burns in oxygen when no **water vapour** is present to form sodium peroxide. And barium reacts with oxygen to form barium peroxide. Metal peroxides are used for bleaching and disinfecting.

Metals and other gases

Some metals also react with other gases. For example, copper roofs often have a green coating. This coating is copper **carbonate**. It is formed by the reaction between copper, water and carbon dioxide in the air. Silver does not react with oxygen in the air. But it does react with hydrogen **sulphide** in the air. This makes the silver **tarnish** with a dark coating.

Red statue

The Statue of Liberty stands at the entrance to New York harbour. Although she was made of shiny, reddish copper, she now looks rather dull and quite green. When the statue was restored between 1984 and 1986, the green coating was not removed. It protects the copper under it from further corrosion.

oxidize   react with oxygen to form an oxide
peroxide   oxide of an element with an extra oxygen atom

Recycling metals

Recycling aluminium

- Recycling one aluminium can saves an amount of energy equal to half that can full of petrol. This is enough energy to run a television for 3 hours.
- Making new cans from recycled aluminium is cheaper, easier and uses 95 per cent less energy than making the cans from aluminium ore.
- Only 42 per cent of the aluminium cans sold in the UK are recycled.

Metals are usually made from **ores**. The ores need to be mined and transported to **smelting** plants. These processes use a lot of energy. If we **recycle** metals we can save a lot of energy. Recycling can also reduce the need for mining and it can save **landfill** space.

Most of the ore deposits that people mine were formed by processes that took millions of years. Those processes are still happening today. But it will take millions of years to replace the ores we have already used. Ores are **non-renewable** resources. Someday the Earth's supply of ores will run out. So recycling will make our supply of metals last longer.

If a car body was just melted down, it would be difficult to separate the iron and steel from the other metals.

Word bank   landfill   place where waste and rubbish are buried

Recycling iron and steel from cars

Every year millions of cars end up in scrapyards. Recycling cars is a challenge because there are so many different materials in them.

The average passenger car contains:

- more than 700 kg of **steel**
- 180 kg of iron
- 100 kg of plastics
- 70 kg of aluminium
- 60 kg of rubber
- 20 kg of copper
- 50 kg of other materials.

After fluids and reusable parts are removed, the car is crushed and fed into a huge shredder. Giant magnets separate the iron and steel from other metals. The iron and steel can then be used to make more steel. Other, less valuable, materials are usually burned or taken to a landfill.

Separating metals

Many recycling centres collect aluminium drinks-cans and steel food-cans in the same bins. Later, strong magnets can be used to separate the two kinds of cans. This is because the iron in steel is magnetic while aluminium is not.

This magnet is separating iron and steel from other materials in a scrapyard.

Find out more

Organizations

The Royal Institute of Great Britain: Inside Out

Science information and resources for young people. Includes quizzes, amazing facts, discussion forums and games.
insideout.rigb.org

New Scientist

Magazine and website with all the latest developments in technology and science. Includes web links for young people.
newscientist.com

BBC Science

News, features and activities on all aspects of science.
bbc.co.uk/science

Books

Iron and the Trace Elements, Jean F. Blashfield (Raintree, 2002)
Marie Curie, Liz Gogerly (Raintree, 2002)
Materials and Processes, Peter D. Riley (Franklin Watts, 1999)
Materials All Around Us, Robert Snedden (Heinemann Library, 2001)

World Wide Web

If you want to find out more about **metals**, you can search the Internet using keywords like these:

- metals + alloys
- 'Bronze Age'
- metals + recycling + [name of your town]
- 'shape memory alloys'
- metals + mining
- [name of a metal] + **properties**
- **elements** + 'periodic table'
- transition metals + KS3

You can also find your own keywords by using headings or words from this book. Use the search tips below to help you find the most useful websites.

Search tips

There are billions of pages on the Internet so it can be difficult to find exactly what you are looking for. For example, if you just type in 'water' on a search engine like Google, you will get a list of 19 million web pages. These search skills will help you find useful websites more quickly:

- Know exactly what you want to find out about first
- Use simple keywords instead of whole sentences
- Use two to six keywords in a search, putting the most important words first
- Be precise – only use names of people, places or things
- If you want to find words that go together, put quote marks around them, for example 'periodic table' or 'transition metals'
- Use the advanced section of your search engine
- Use the + sign to add certain words, for example typing + KS3 into the search box will help you find web pages at the right level.

Where to search

Search engine

A search engine looks through the entire web and lists all the sites that match the words in the search box. They can give thousands of links, but the best matches are at the top of the list, on the first page. Try **bbc.co.uk/search**

Search directory

A search directory is more like a library of websites that have been sorted by a person instead of a computer. You can search by keyword or subject and browse through the different sites like you would look through books on a library shelf. A good example is **yahooligans.com**

Glossary

abrasive substance that grinds or polishes a surface

alkali metals group of very reactive metals in Group I of the periodic table

alloy metal formed by mixing together two or more melted metals

arthritis painful, swollen joints

atom smallest particle of an element

boiling point temperature at which a substance changes from a liquid to a gas

Bronze Age period of history from about 3500 B.C.E. to about 1000 B.C.E.

carat measurement of the amount of gold in an alloy

carbonate compound of carbon, oxygen and another element

chemical reaction change that forms one or more new substances with new properties

chemist scientist who studies chemical reactions

chlorophyll green chemical in plants

coke form of carbon made from coal

compound substance made of atoms of two or more different elements

conductor material through which heat or electricity passes easily

corroded damaged by a reaction with air

corrosion damage to the surface of a metal, caused by its reaction with air

crust outer layer of the Earth; we live on the Earth's crust

decay break apart and change to something else

density mass in a given volume of matter; measured in grams per cubic centimetre or kilograms per cubic metre

ductile can be drawn into a wire

electric charge amount of electricity on something

electrolysis using electricity to separate an ore that has been melted

electron tiny, negatively charged particle outside the nucleus of an atom

element substance made of one type of atom

engineer person who works in planning and building things like bridges, buildings and machines

evaporate change from a liquid to a gas

filament thin wire in a light bulb

fluoresce give off light when certain rays strike

foil very thin sheet of metal

galvanized covered with a thin coating of zinc to prevent rusting

gauge unit for measuring thickness of wire

Geiger counter instrument used to measure radioactivity

hoist equipment for lifting up heavy loads

hydroxide compound containing a metal and an oxygen-hydrogen group

insulator material through which heat or electricity does not pass easily

ion atom or group of atoms with an electric charge

landfill place where waste and rubbish are buried

Latin language of ancient Romans

lustre shine that metals have

malleable can be hammered, rolled, or shaped without breaking

magnetic field area around a magnet where its magnetic force is felt

mass amount of matter in an object; measured in grams or kilograms

melting point temperature at which a substance changes from a solid to a liquid

metals group of materials with certain properties

metalloid element with some properties of both metals and non-metals

meteorite chunk of rock and metal from outer space that has crashed on a planet

mineral non-living solid material

native metal metal that is found naturally in its pure form

neutron uncharged particle in the nucleus of an atom

nodule small, rounded lump

non-renewable cannot be replaced once used up

nucleus dense, positively charged centre of an atom

ore metal combined with other elements

oxide compound of oxygen and another element or elements

oxidize react with oxygen to form an oxide

particle bit or piece

periodic table chart in which elements with similar properties are arranged in groups

peroxide oxide of an element with an extra oxygen atom

physical property feature that can be observed without changing what a substance is made of

plating covering with a thin layer of metal

property feature of something

proton positively charged particle in the nucleus of an atom

radioactivity rays or particles given off by a substance

radioactive metal unstable metal whose nucleus breaks down and gives off particles and radiation

reactant something taking part in a chemical reaction

reactive easily takes part in chemical reactions

recycled treated in order to use again

red heat heat at which a material glows red

relay journey where an object is carried by more than one person

roasting heating an ore in air to produce an oxide

rods very thick wires

shaft vertical hole in the ground

shape memory alloy alloy that returns to its original shape when heated

smelting separating a metal from its ore using heat

solder alloy that can be melted and used to join or mend metal parts

steel alloy of iron with a small amount of carbon added; some steel also contains small amounts of other metals

strands very thin wires

sulphide compound of sulphur and another element

tarnish make dull by a reaction with air

tensile strength property of a metal that stops it from being torn apart

toxic poisonous

unstable capable of decay

ultraviolet light invisible part of light from the sun; also given off by a 'black light'

vein crack in rock filled with a metal or an ore

water vapour water in the form of a gas

Index